Real Estate Career Path Guide!

Real Estate Career Path Guide!

Randal S. Doaty

Copyright © 2018 by Randal S. Doaty.

ISBN: Softcover   978-1-9845-6486-3
           eBook   978-1-9845-6485-6

All rights reserved. No part of this book may be reproduced or transmitted in any form or by any means, electronic or mechanical, including photocopying, recording, or by any information storage and retrieval system, without permission in writing from the copyright owner.

The views expressed in this work are solely those of the author and do not necessarily reflect the views of the publisher, and the publisher hereby disclaims any responsibility for them.

Any people depicted in stock imagery provided by Getty Images are models, and such images are being used for illustrative purposes only.
Certain stock imagery © Getty Images.

Print information available on the last page.

Rev. date: 11/06/2018

To order additional copies of this book, contact:
Xlibris
1-888-795-4274
www.Xlibris.com
Orders@Xlibris.com
787839

CONTENTS

Foreword vii

Chapter 1	Donna's Path	1
Chapter 2	What's This Book All About?	5
Chapter 3	Knowledge, Skills & Tools	8
Chapter 4	Five Major Career Steps	12
Chapter 5	Four Real Estate Sales Roles	18
Chapter 6	Today's Solo Real Estate Agent	20
Chapter 7	Real Estate Partnerships	22
Chapter 8	Real Estate Teams	25
Chapter 9	Real Estate Groups	27
Chapter 10	Commission Splits Changed Real Estate	30
Chapter 11	Choosing Wide or Deep	33
Chapter 12	Part-Time and Limited-Service Agents	36
Chapter 13	The Missing Parts	39
Chapter 14	Who Needs A License Anyway?	41
Chapter 15	The Problem-Solving Business	44
Chapter 16	Curiosity for Sale	46
Chapter 17	Do You Use An S-GPS?	49
Chapter 18	The Spectrum Networks	52
Chapter 19	Where Do We Go from Here?	55

FOREWORD

Welcome to the *Real Estate Career Path Guide*! This book is not available for sale to the public. We selectively target our readers, and we have selected you!

You received a copy of our book because you possess certain qualities that are of interest to us! We hope to start a conversation with you about various industry topics that are relevant to all our career paths. We would like your personal feedback and insights about these concepts!

We will introduce some new and innovative real estate career perspectives for you to consider. Whether you are just starting in real estate, have been selling for years, or you are retiring from this business, there is something in these pages for everyone.

I have been a salesman, broker, manager and a real estate company owner. I'm also a state-licensed real estate instructor, teacher, trainer, mentor, coach, career counselor and sales role matchmaker. This book is based on my 30-year journey, as well as some valuable insight from the influential real estate professionals I have met along my path.

One of those influential people was Donna Russell. This book appropriately begins with a glimpse at Donna's real estate career path. Her story and many of the concepts and philosophies in this book should help you navigate your own journey through the maze of real estate pathways.

I promise this publication will be a worthwhile reading experience!

Randal S. Doaty,
Real Estate Career Path Guide

CHAPTER 1

Donna's Path

In 1991 I was at a picnic at my cousin's house in Gilbertsville. There I had the good fortune to meet Chris and Donna Russell. I was actively selling real estate back in those days. Chris and Donna were hoping to sell their home on Edgewood Street in Pottstown to be able to buy their dream home in New Hanover Township. They asked for my help.

The Russells had already identified the home they wanted to purchase, and they had also found the buyer for their home in Pottstown on their own. There was little for me to do other than assist them with the paperwork and help navigate some of the logistics of the sale and purchase of both properties.

I was the co-owner of Herb & Doaty Realtors when I met Donna Russell. In addition to real estate sales, I actively recruited and trained new real estate agents. Most of the prospective agents back then contacted our company with the hope and dream of selling real estate. That's not what happened with Donna. As she puts it, I hounded her to get into real estate!

For nearly two years after Chris and Donna purchased their new home, I continued to maintain contact and plant seeds, encouraging Donna to become a full-time real estate agent. She had what it takes, and I knew it immediately. I recognized something in her that she didn't see in herself – she was a real estate superstar in waiting!

Donna certainly didn't lack confidence or charm. She was a high-energy individual with a bubbly personality. Donna's communications spectrum was also amazing. She was as comfortable talking to a CEO in the boardroom as she was a biker in the bar room. Her laugh and smile were contagious, and she sincerely cared about other people. She had a big heart back then, and she still does today!

The notion of selling real estate captured Donna's imagination from the start, but there was a problem. Donna worked at another full-time job and she carried the health insurance for the entire family. Making a move into real estate sales meant leaving the security of a regular paycheck and good benefits. Living on real estate commissions alone was frightening.

This risk was also a two-way street for me. Donna and Chris had become friends. If Donna failed at real estate, I would feel terrible. I knew the financial risk she and her family would be taking. Industry statistics show that more than 85% of those who attempt a full-time career in real estate will fail. I knew those frightening odds!

Donna's personality and character were a real plus when it came to the likelihood of her sales success, but I also knew that wouldn't be enough. I had seen others just like her fail at real estate sales. She needed more. Donna had three other things that I believe were, and still are, the secret sauce behind her successful real estate sales career.

In the following chapters, I will outline the three essential ingredients for real estate sales: knowledge, skills and tools. From the very start, it was obvious to me that Donna Russell had an insatiable appetite to learn every aspect of the real estate business. Her thirst for knowledge, efforts to develop skills and commitment to acquire the best tools made her unique.

It has been 25 years since Donna Russell was first licensed. She could write her own book about real estate experiences at this point. While I was writing this book, I was also teaching a class for new real estate recruits. Donna asked me if I would be offering any new material in my class. I told her I was. Donna Russell still attends many of my classes today!

Donna's career path has taken her places she never imagined she would go in terms of sales performance. I attribute this to the fact that she is both teachable and coachable. She is a perpetual student of the arts and sciences of real estate sales – learning, unlearning and relearning as needed. But event more importantly, she is open to taking direction and advice!

Early in Donna's career, she had become very proficient at selling smaller homes in Pottstown. She realized she had reached a performance plateau and wanted to break into a new marketplace. I explained there are two ways to double your income in real estate. You can either sell twice as many homes or sell homes that are worth twice as much.

Although my last comment may seem obvious, it isn't easy to do. Donna allowed me to help her break into new marketplaces while continuing to serve the niche market she had developed in Pottstown. My direction and advice would have been totally useless if Donna hadn't been open to my instruction. I still remember how her income soared in later years.

In Chapter 17, I will share about the S-GPS, which I personally created for real estate sales. This system was the launchpad for my own sales career, and Donna used my system to help her get off the ground, as well. She followed the system exactly as it was designed. She allowed me and the S-GPS to be her sales trainer and performance quantification system.

Donna had a natural inclination for sales and marketing. She knew how to build identity in the marketplace. In the mid to late 1990s, I created TV54, which was a local cable television channel exclusively for Herb & Doaty Realtors that reached more 300,000 viewers in our region. None of my agents used this advertising tool better than Donna Russell.

Donna is good in front of a camera – she's a natural. Her real estate video walk-thru productions became her trademark while cable television was still in its prime. She became the familiar face of local real estate. Her clients explained to me that they liked Donna even before they met her in person because of her TV persona. This medium served her well.

I don't take credit for Donna's success. Everything I just explained about Donna illustrates the importance of what an agent needs to bring to the table and what the broker or manager must provide. The dynamic relationship between gifted sales people and those who guide their career path is truly vital. The people along your path are very important!

I have been through major career steps with Donna. She has allowed me to be her teacher, instructor, trainer, mentor, coach and career counselor. It is my honor to still work beside Donna after 25 years. One of the great blessings in my real estate career was to watch her soar to her full real estate sales potential. And all the success truly belongs to her!

What success? In the past two and half decades, Donna Russell has had more than $150 million dollars in real estate sales here in the tri-county area. Donna was the top producing agent at Re/Max Achievers in 2017, and she is consistently in one of the top performing sales levels in our company year after year. She is reliably a top producer.

Even more impressive than her sales is the fact that Donna has done it all while giving outstanding customer service, earning the respect of her real estate peers, and serving her community, while still being an incredible mom and a loving wife. She has maintained balance, character and poise as a real estate professional and has not lost sight of what is most important.

Few have done real estate sales better than Donna Russell!

CHAPTER 2

What's This Book All About?

When I began writing "Real Estate Career Paths," it started as a brochure for real estate agents in our marketplace. I consulted with other trusted real estate professionals about these business concepts. Each conversation raised new and interesting perspectives. We at Re/Max Achievers thought this material might be of interest to you.

My 30-year career in real estate has been filled with great people like Donna Russell. I have had interesting experiences that have generated some unique perspectives about the past, present and future of the real estate industry. But I am equally interested in your thoughts! This book will grow and expand in subsequent editions with your input.

One of the biggest revelations during my peer discussions was a noticeable lack of uniform vocabulary to define important terms along our career paths. This book offers some fresh, new terminology about our career steps, education, newly emerging sales collaboratives and more. I guarantee you will learn terminology you have never heard before.

The real estate industry is a complex maze of real estate roles and relationships that are constantly changing. It's easy to get lost and possible to get stuck. This book was written to serve as a useful tool for people who are looking for direction or understanding and for those who are hungry to learn more about the real estate industry.

I will occasionally refer to the old days of real estate but not merely to reflect on days gone by. To understand real estate today and the real estate industry of tomorrow, we need to understand how we got here. There are some valuable lessons from our real estate past that can help us understand and navigate the winding path ahead.

This book was written specifically for the real estate professionals in our Pennsylvania marketplace. We don't intend to sell this book on the Internet or in book stores. It was specifically written for real estate agents practicing in southeastern Pennsylvania. It was written for you.

My role at Re/Max Achievers is to serve as a teacher, instructor, trainer, coach, mentor, career counselor and sales matchmaker. I am always on the lookout for quality individuals to complement our partnerships, teams and a newly formed group. I actively seek great sales collaborative matches!

Throughout my real estate career, I have also been recruited. I'm amazed how desperately these folks wanted me to move my license to their firm, yet they knew so little about me. They were interested in my sales volume or they knew I could afford to pay their high desk rental. How touching?!

A recruiter will try to convince you to join their company. A matchmaker helps you fit into the right sales role or collaborative relationships within their company. There is a big difference! A recruiter sells everything they have to offer. A matchmaker wants to know you better and they truly listen to what you are saying.

I consider myself to be a real estate role matchmaker, like I shared in the story of Donna Russell. A good match occurs when two sides fit well together. This book will help you understand our side at Re/Max Achievers. Maybe you would be a good match, or maybe not. That's not the point of this book. More important is your personal feedback!

This book is being shared with real estate professionals who have been in the industry for decades. It is also offered to real estate career hopefuls with little or no experience whatsoever. This allows Re/Max Achievers to maintain a dialog with a wide range of people offering a very broad perspective about these topics.

Many who read this book may be quite happy where they are currently working. That's great! We aren't trying to lure you away from a real estate firm that is offering everything you need. It would be selfish of us, and ridiculous for you, to give up a strong working relationship. If you are already at a good company with great co-workers - stay there!

As you read on, some of the chapters may not seem relevant to you. Trust me, every topic relates in one way or another to all of us, regardless of our tenure in this business. I encourage you to read every chapter. This entire book can be read in less than two hours. If you go through and cherry-pick topics, you will miss some very important points.

When you are finished reading this book, please feel free to share it with others who might benefit from these words. This book will be helpful to those who are considering a new career in real estate. If someone you know is right for the real estate business, like Donna Russell, this book will offer some valuable insight for them to consider.

I hope you enjoy our *Real Estate Career Path Guide*. We've shared our thoughts with you. We sincerely hope you will share your thoughts with us, too! You can reach me directly at rdoaty@doaty.com.

CHAPTER 3

Knowledge, Skills & Tools

If you don't have adequate knowledge, proficient skills and the proper tools in real estate, you are destined for failure in this industry. This may seem like a harsh statement with which to begin a book, but it's the absolute truth. These three things will be your foundation for success. The fact that you passed your state licensure exam means virtually nothing!

Success in the real estate industry belongs to those who are committed, career-long learners! Everything you know and understand today in real estate isn't necessarily useful tomorrow. The exponential growth of technology, social networking, communications and our evolving business practices change daily!

Navigating the five big career steps that will be covered in the next chapter requires constant access to good educational resources. The right blend of teaching, instructing, training, mentoring, coaching and career counseling can transform an ordinary agent into an extraordinary agent. Education adds "extra" to the ordinary!

Your real estate career path is a journey that requires knowledge, skills and tools. If you lack any of these three, you will get lost or become stuck. Your real estate education will take you to places you want to go and help get you out of the places where you feel trapped. You will need to leverage every form of education to succeed in this business.

Knowledge is the foundation upon which your career must be built. A knowledgeable real estate agent can build a career that will withstand every type of market condition and calamity. This book is a form of real estate education. It won't teach you how to sell real estate, but it will equip you to practice real estate differently and to become a better salesperson.

Real estate sales requires certain skills. These skills are developed through instruction, practice and repetition. When skills are not used on a regular basis, they can quickly diminish. Successful sales professionals need to be skilled salespeople. The skills we must learn need to be taught by qualified and experienced educators.

If you have the knowledge and the skills but lack the proper tools, you are still not fully equipped for real estate sales. These tools consist of tangible products and software, but they can also include systems and techniques needed to accomplish certain tasks. You must have a fully stocked sales toolbox to build a successful real estate career.

The following six different forms of real estate education were essential elements along my career path. They enhanced my professional development. As you progress along your own career path, make sure you have access to each of these uniquely different educational resources. Without these, you will lack the necessary knowledge, skills and tools to succeed in real estate sales.

TEACHER – a real estate *teacher* provides a "*broad view*" of the big picture of the real estate industry. You must understand both the art and science of selling homes. Agents need to master real estate mathematics, history, philosophy, law, marketing, psychology, engineering and much more. A teacher provides a comprehensive understanding of our industry, which gives us the right to call ourselves real estate *professionals*.

INSTRUCTOR – a real estate *instructor* provides instruction to master specific tasks or use of professional tools. Instructors help you "*focus*" on specific sales practices and disciplines. When you are learning how to use the MLS, prepare a CMA, write a contract, choose an addendum, calculate tax appeals, etc., you need an experienced *instructor* to guide you. An *instructor* will help you build and expand your professional sales skill toolbox.

TRAINER – a real estate *trainer* will "*push you*" as an individual and strengthen your sales muscles to reach your peak performance, just like a physical trainer in a gym. They employ systems to show us measurable growth like the real estate sales GPS program I describe in Chapter 17. Trainers help us reach the next step in our performance plateaus. A trainer will help you reach performance goals you could not otherwise reach on your own.

MENTOR – a real estate *mentor* is a transaction partner and monitor who acts as a second set of eyes. They supplement your on-the-job training by sharing their "*insight and experience*" as you practice real estate under their guidance. They are the voice of real life experience and share transactional expertise. Whether you are watching them do business or they are watching you do business, they can help. Also understand that not every top producer will also be a great mentor!

COACH – a real estate *coach* helps us build partnerships, teams and groups to maximize the collective energies of all the participants. They are "*human chemistry*" experts who understand how to harness the collective power of the individual parts that result in successful real estate collaboratives. A trainer works with individuals, whereas a coach helps multiple people work together. Coaches are an essential resource for building and growing collaboratives!

CAREER COUNSELOR – a real estate *career counselor* provides guidance for individuals and collaboratives making important career decisions. They are real estate career path experts. They offer the voice of experience and provide a sounding board for major career path decisions. They should also be career match-makers who are willing to get to know you – not ordinary recruiters who are paid to entice you to join their firm.

As you progress down the path through your real estate career, you will need someone to serve as your Teacher, Instructor, Trainer, Mentor, Coach and Career Counselor. These roles don't need to be filled by six different people, but they need to be offered by dedicated educators who understand their purpose, as well as you and your unique role.

When you have finished real estate school and passed your licensure exam, your education isn't over – it's just beginning. If you intend to be in this profession for many years, the process of learning, unlearning and re-learning is just beginning. When you finally stop learning in the real estate business, your career has officially ended!

CHAPTER 4

Five Major Career Steps

I have served in many roles in real estate over the past three decades. These roles have prepared me to become a real estate career counselor. If you hope to find success along your career path, you will need someone with experience who can provide direction for your journey. There are definitely major career obstacles ahead. I call them "career steps".

I have identified five major steps you could potentially face. Each of these steps must be carefully considered. Whether you are just starting your career, improving your career, pausing your career, returning to your career or ending your real estate journey, you will probably have some major decisions ahead. Each step offers a unique challenge!

Stepping INTO Real Estate

Unlicensed Roles

A real estate license is not required to work in this industry. Some tasks need to be performed by a licensed real estate professional. Many do not! If you want to work in real estate, you must understand which services require a real estate license and what tasks can be performed legally by a non-licensee. The real estate industry has very strict laws!

Unlicensed roles include "administrative assistant" and "real estate technician". Many tasks that are administrative or technical in nature are still an essential part of the real estate sales process. These unlicensed roles will be explained in more detail later in this book. But yes, you can work in real estate without having a license!

Limited-Service Licensee Roles

Not everyone with a real estate license wants to or is able to perform every function that is permitted by licensure regulations. Nor should they! A Limited-Service Licensee only performs certain tasks, and they work in tandem with Full-Service Licensees. It's a bad decision to work part-time in an industry that deserves your full attention.

Persons serving as a "Limited-Service Licensee" act as showing hosts, open house hosts, referral agents and more. They serve in this capacity because they don't have the time or experience to properly service clients or their peers as a solo agent. This role is a great way to get started in real estate and learn the ropes.

Full-Service Licensee Roles

If you want to be considered a true professional, you should be a "Full-Service Licensee". These folks make real estate their full-time priority. They are committed to career-long learning and customer service. They actively list and sell real estate with frequency, which allows them to be proficient in most of the home sales skills.

If you are unable to fulfill the lofty standards of being a "Full-Service Licensee" individually, you could also do it collectively. Collaborative sales relationships are another option to consider if you can't offer Full-Services by yourself. Real estate consumers and your peers deserve your full attention. Collaboratives are explained in more detail in later chapters.

The first step is a big step! Careful consideration of your new role in real estate is essential. When you are looking for a place to hang your new license, make sure you understand the specific role you hope to play, and be sure your new office supports that role. And remember, not every real estate company is staffed to help those who are just starting in sales!

Stepping UP in Real Estate

The next major step in your real estate career will be an achievement plateau. Humans are creatures of habit, so we continue to do the same things whether we realize it or not. Our patterned behavior is evidenced each time we reach a sales productivity plateau. We keep earning the same, because we keep doing the same.

Change isn't easy, but that's exactly what is required to reach the next level of productivity. If you want your income to change, either the way you practice real estate or the way you live your life will need to be altered. Most of us cannot implement measurable change by ourselves or without help from a professional sales trainer.

Real estate sales require a tremendous amount of our time and energy. This time and energy must come from somewhere, and sometimes it is stolen from our personal and family life. This theft of energy can have a negative effect on us physically, emotionally and relationally as we pursue these elusive achievement plateaus.

If you choose to climb to new financial heights, you will need someone to help monitor your ascent. I have watched great agents rise to amazing sales productivity heights and then suddenly burn out. Their desire to sell real estate quickly dwindled, and their personal life was devastated.

It's possible to have the best of both worlds but not by doing things the way they have always been done. A real estate career must be carefully engineered to handle increased speed and altitude, just like an aircraft. There is no reason to crash and burn if you can get qualified help from a career counselor or sales trainer.

The "next plateau" is the second big step you are likely to face along the career path. Each new sales performance plateau brings financial rewards, but it also poses new risks to consider. Not everyone is drawn to these lofty financial heights. That's OKAY! You can choose to remain at the financial plateau that works best for you and your family!

Stepping AWAY from Real Estate

Sometimes we need to step away from real estate sales. Life can throw some difficult circumstances our way. Sales performance relies on sharp cognitive skills. When calamity strikes, our ability to service sales clients can be compromised, and we may no longer function effectively as sales professionals.

Over the years I have counseled top performing agents who faced the loss of a loved one, divorce, financial calamities, health battles, disabilities, lawsuits and much more. It was devastating to them and their families and sometimes their careers. There is hope! The clouds will eventually lift, and you will see your career path clearly again.

These unfortunate seasons in our lifetime can be career-ending if not handled properly. Life isn't the same following a tragedy, and business can't be handled the same when we are caught in life's stormy seas. These challenges can be managed professionally and with the assistance of someone who understands.

Your current customers and clients may be understanding when a life crisis suddenly occurs, but it is unreasonable to think new customers would be willing to accept your limited professional abilities. These folks are paying for a professional service, and they are entitled to it. Your business pipeline is at risk, and it can come to a screeching halt.

Some of your fellow agents in the office may be willing to help for a while. You would probably do the same for them. Sadly, these arrangements can outlast their welcome, especially if the unfortunate life calamity has long-term implications. But there is hope if you get the right support!

Stepping away from real estate is a very difficult and complicated step, but it can be done. It can be accomplished through the assistance of a career counselor who is familiar with these situations. Don't allow your real estate career to simply collapse because of unfortunate life circumstances. Get the help you need!

Stepping BACK INTO Real Estate

If you have stepped away from real estate for one reason or another, the time may come when you want to step back into your career. If you think you are just going to just pick up where you left off, you may be sadly mistaken. Depending on how long you have been gone, you could be entering a whole new world.

The ever-changing nature of the real estate industry makes it hard to pick up where you left off. You will be facing new technologies, unfamiliar paperwork, changing laws and consumers who look at real estate professionals differently. It can be intimidating when everything you once knew about this business seems to have changed.

A return to the real estate marketplace is something that needs to be carefully planned with someone who understands the re-entry process. It's not just about learning what is new; it's also about deprogramming a sales mindset that may no longer be relevant in today's real estate marketplace.

This step is not only a challenge for folks who have been away for many years. If you have stepped away to handle a personal tragedy, your re-entry into real estate sales can be difficult after only a few months. Your cognitive abilities may have been altered by the trauma of your circumstance. You can face motivational and focus challenges.

Whether you needed a break, were raising a family, or you are trying to adjust to post-traumatic sales, the jump back into the real estate marketplace will require some coaching, counseling and training assistance. Re-entry can be tricky, and the process is uniquely different for everyone.

Some of the new roles in real estate, as well as the opportunities offered by real estate sales collaboratives, are alternatives you can consider. As you continue to read this guide, you will come across various opportunities that could fit your current circumstance. Don't make a career-ending decision before speaking to someone who can help you.

Stepping OUT of Real Estate

How does one retire from real estate sales? Most real estate agents simply stop returning phone calls or tell friends, family and past clients they are no longer practicing real estate. Everything they invested to build their proverbial book of business could quickly dwindle down to nothing. If you want to preserve what you have built, you will need help.

If you are a successful real estate professional, you have surely built a good reputation and following. The people in your database lean upon your opinion and perspective above all others. They also tend to trust the people you trust. There is value in your reputation, as well as the contacts in your database. Don't just throw them all away!

Safely landing a real estate career is like landing an aircraft. It isn't as easy as it looks! It will require careful calculations and the assistance of people who are skilled at this process. You are entitled to residual income for all the time and energy you have invested. Yet, many fail miserably at this final step.

The Steps Ahead

The first and the last step I described are inevitable – a beginning and an end. We need to calculate how we will get into the real estate business and how we will eventually leave real estate sales permanently. How we start and how we finish our career path is important. I suggest talking with a real estate career counselor.

You may or may not face the middle three steps. If you are content with your sales performance or life doesn't throw you any serious challenges, your career could move ahead smoothly. I hope this is the case. However, it's important to know help is available through a real estate career counselor if you encounter these obstacles along your path.

I serve as the real estate career counselor at Re/Max Achievers. When you interview with other real estate offices, it is important to understand who will fill this role in their company. Inquire about their qualifications and tenure in real estate. The failure rate is high among new real estate recruits. I attribute this to a serious lack of career counseling.

If you take one thing away from this book, I hope it is a clear understanding of the career steps you could face one day. Whether you are with Re/Max Achievers or elsewhere, don't hesitate to contact me. We cooperate with the commissions we share, so we can certainly cooperate with each other when it involves making these key career decisions.

CHAPTER 5

Four Real Estate Sales Roles

You need to recognize the four primary sales roles. Each of these roles has their own unique characteristics that will be described in more detail in following chapters. The descriptions I offer in this chapter will enhance your real estate sales vocabulary. We need this understanding to have meaningful conversations about our career paths.

If there is one term used in this book more than any other, it is "collaborative". This term simply means two or more parties working together. Although the concept of collaboration is simple, its application in real estate business is much more complex. I believe sales collaboratives represent the future of this industry.

If you are a solo agent, I am not suggesting you are on the real estate sales endangered species list. Even if you have no intention of joining a real estate collaborative at this point in your career, I encourage you to keep reading what I have to say. You need to understand this new breed that already has or will soon be invading your marketplace.

The terms "partnership," "team" and "group" have been used interchangeably in the real estate industry for decades. They are not the same as collaboration! These sales styles have different purposes and operational characteristics. Each sales style exists for entirely different reasons. This is important for you to know!

Solo – A "solo" real estate agent operates as a single sales entity. They do all aspects of sales themselves. Some may employ administrative assistants for extra help. They often have a confident personality and prefer to do things themselves. They want to know things are done right. Many real estate agents in the industry today operate as solo agents. There are benefits and downsides to doing sales alone!

Partnership - A real estate "partnership" is a mutually beneficial and symbiotic relationship between two or more partners. Each participant maintains their own identity, yet they work together and share workloads to achieve the desired lifestyle or financial goals. Some of the strongest partnerships do not necessarily consist of like-kind people. A left-brain and a right-brain can make a whole brain!

Team – Look at a real estate "team" as a sports metaphor. Each member has a specific role and they contribute their own areas of expertise. Participants must have a unique purpose and work efficiently with all the other parts. Teams work to build the identity and brand of the whole team or the lead agent, unlike a partnership or a group. They are designed to run efficiently like a sales-generating machine.

Group - A "group" is like a company within a company. These entities consist of combinations of solo agents and all types of collaboratives. A group works to harness the collective energy of all the members, for the benefit of all, and thereby increases their own service offerings in the marketplace. The biggest benefit of a real estate group is their combined level and diverse range of overall real estate expertise.

An important function of today's real estate broker or office manager is to assist with the development of these new age sales collaboratives. Supporting solo sales agents, as well as building partnerships, teams and groups, requires the knowledge and experience of those who understand the science of collaborative real estate sales.

Only you can decide which role is best suited for your personality and lifestyle. The sales role that is best for each of us depends on where we are on our career path. It can change when we face one of the five major career steps in Chapter 4. Knowing which role is best for you also requires the six forms of real estate education to make your decision!

As you read my description of the real estate sales roles in the following chapters, please understand I am not trying to convince you to choose one role over another. The right sales role at the right point in your career will be your choice. I don't know you – yet. I only ask that you keep an open mind to all the sales role options I am about to describe.

CHAPTER 6

Today's Solo Real Estate Agent

Solo agency was the only way real estate was practiced in 1988 when I started my real estate career. It was a different world back then. Most of the folks selling real estate were full-time salespeople, and the agreement of sale was just two pages long. Everyone worked for the Seller – no buyer agency – let the buyer beware!

Some of us who launched our real estate careers before Y2K are increasingly frustrated as we try to do business as we once did. But the notion of partnerships, teams and groups also seems foreign to us – it's just not the way we have been comfortable selling homes.

Some of the best agents I have ever known, like Donna Russel, were solo agents, and many of them are still practicing real estate today. Solo salespeople still have their own place in the real estate sales eco-system. They have built solid careers through hard work, and they continued to learn so they can adapt to this ever-changing industry. I applaud them!

Selling real estate is much more complex today. There is far more paperwork. Checklists are long, and we have a calendar filled with critical dates for every single transaction. It's a logistical juggling act. Not everyone has the multi-tasking personality needed to deal with all these responsibilities by themselves.

An administrative assistant or real estate technician is a useful tool for solo agents who find themselves overwhelmed by real estate. Sometimes getting a little extra help can make a big difference. Finding someone who can fill your weaknesses with their strengths is the key to sales success. If you are struggling as a solo agent, there is help available!

The advent of real estate sales collaboratives has now changed the playing field for solo agents. Although a solo sales style may be right for your personality and lifestyle, real estate consumers are getting smarter. Savvy consumers are asking tougher questions that were never asked when everyone was acting as a solo real estate practitioner.

After 30 years in the real estate industry, I question whether I would hire a solo real estate agent, myself. Even the best agents in the industry can become overwhelmed when the market gets crazy or they encounter difficult life circumstances. Just knowing an agent has partners, team members or group affiliates is comforting to me.

Increasingly, consumers want to hear about your sales back-up plan if you expect them to sign an exclusive buyer or seller agency contract. It's a fair question! Why should consumers be legally bound to a solo agent for several months if the agent is rendered ineffective for one reason or another? Collaboratives offer consumers more assurance.

Our industry also has a generation of solo real estate agents who are ready to retire. Working alone may have been great up to this point, but it probably won't be a viable career exit strategy. It's better to become part of a partnership, team or group than allow all your hard work to simply dwindle to nothing.

If you suddenly stop selling real estate and refer your customers and clients to someone they don't know, your real estate book of business is going to die a quick death. It seems like it would work, but it doesn't. Until the advent of real estate collaboratives, those wanting to retire from real estate had limited retirement choices. That's not true anymore!

The move out of real estate sales needs to be a carefully calculated transition. Solo agents may have to consider the unthinkable! Your last years in real estate could include developing a relationship with a collaborative. If you want to retain your identity, become part of a partnership or group. If your identity isn't important anymore, join a team.

A real estate group may be the best option of all, but a true group isn't easy to find in this region. Re/Max Achievers has a real estate group solution that allows seasoned agents the option to phase out of real estate sales at a very comfortable pace. You can read more about groups in Chapter 9.

If solo real estate sales are working for you, then keep doing it that way! If you are just totally overwhelmed or getting ready to retire from real estate, you need to seriously consider one of the collaborative arrangements that are described in more detail in the next few chapters.

CHAPTER 7

Real Estate Partnerships

Real estate *"partnerships"* were the first generation in the sales evolution process as agents started looking for a solution to solo sales. A partnership consists of two or more agents who want to share a mutually beneficial and symbiotic working relationship. These agents also want to retain the independence and identity of a solo sales style.

Real estate partnerships do not focus on building the identity of the partnership in the marketplace. Each member retains and promotes their own identity with consumers. But they boldly promote the fact they work together as a partnership to help them overcome the concerns that some consumers may have regarding working with solo agents.

Partnerships allow members to share duties with each other when additional help is needed. They share resources and expertise. A partnership demands a higher level of accountability to meet sales performance goals. Partners work independently, but they do not compete against each other for business because of the relationship.

The strongest partnerships are a merger of uniquely different people who can each bring something to the relationship. An example would be when seasoned agents who know and understand the real estate business work with less experienced agents who better understand newer technology and social media. They are able to balance each other.

The financial arrangements of partnerships vary widely. Some partners each keep what they earn, but they may share some expenses mutually. Other partnerships divide the net sales income and expenses equally. The personalities of the people in the partnership, along with their sales performance levels, usually determine how the money is handled.

A partnership with multiple members might appear to be a "team". They could even refer to themselves as being a team. So how do you know the difference? A real estate team is an identity-building, high performance sales machine. A partnership is merely a collaboration of solo agents. You will learn more about the core characteristics of a team in the next chapter.

Business partnerships are prone to failure. They can start out on a happy note but sour quickly when goals, values and personal interests conflict. We all change over time, and the people in a partnership may not all evolve in the same direction. You should discuss an exit strategy from the start. A partnership can become a battleship and then quickly a sinking ship!

Partnerships, like all real estate collaboratives, rely upon the right combination and balance of people. They must be built and designed thoughtfully. Rules and expectations should be clearly outlined from the start. Partnerships are the most volatile of all the collaboratives because of the identity retention nature of this relationship.

Some agents realize they need to do something, but they just don't know what they need to do. Ask yourself these simple questions if you are considering a partnership.

- Am I willing to be accountable to other people for my personal investment of time and money into this partnership?
- Am I willing to trust other people to do their fair share of the work in this business relationship and speak up when they don't?
- Am I willing to accept others will handle business in ways that are different from me and be able to accept these differences?
- Am I willing to invest the time to lay the ground rules and expectation of all partners to engineer this relationship from the very start?
- Am I willing to seek professional help and guidance to try to build a partnership that could be a lasting business relationship?

If the answer to any of these five questions is "NO", you should continue working as a solo agent. Real estate partnerships are only a wise choice for individuals who are capable of working in a symbiotic and sometimes imperfectly balanced business relationship.

If you are considering a sales partnership, it would be wise for everyone to meet with a real estate career counselor. It can be helpful having an experienced, independent third party helping to lay the groundwork for this new relationship. It is like getting pre-marital counseling. It's definitely worthwhile!

We have several successful real estate partnerships at Re/Max Achievers. My daughter is in one of those business relationships. She is in the right place, at the right time. Her sales partner is a seasoned sales professional who I recruited and trained myself. They give real estate sales partnerships a good name. I am proud of both of them!

If you are thinking about shifting from solo sales to a partnership, or if the real estate team relationship isn't working, we should talk. Real estate sales partnerships have plenty to offer, and the real estate consumers of today may look at you differently when they can see you have a back-up plan to serve their needs!

CHAPTER 8

Real Estate Teams

This chapter focuses entirely on real estate sales teams. They are the hot topic in the real estate industry today. As you've learned so far, the solo real estate sales model eventually morphed into real estate partnerships. The next step in the evolutionary process occurred when agents realized they could become sales machines.

A true real estate team has an entirely different mindset than those in a real estate partnership. On a team, each component is dependent upon the smooth operation of the other components. If one part of the machine isn't running efficiently, the entire machine probably isn't working properly. Each member of a team has a purpose.

Wearing the same color shirt with a name printed on the back doesn't create a baseball team. The same is true of a real estate team. Every member of the team has a key position to fill and a role they will play in the sales game. When a position isn't filled or is left open, the whole team is likely to suffer.

The best way to build a team is to hire a real estate coach. They understand the chemistry of teamwork. It's logical to believe a group of top producers would make the perfect team. That's not true in either sports or real estate sales. It's nice to have top producers, but they also need to fit into the overall game plan for your marketplace.

One of the first things I teach new agents is something I created called "The Heart of Real Estate". I use the analogy of a 3-chamber heart to describe the real estate sales process. When I am building or consulting with a team, I use another illustration describing the five cogs needed to build an effective real estate team sales machine.

The first cog is the marketing and advertising cog. The next is the prospect management and development cog. This is followed by the marketplace cog, which then leads into the transaction cog. The final and fifth cog is the reinvestment cog. Any team that has someone working in each of these key positions is destined for success.

In a baseball game, where players are placed on the field is important. You can't just stand anywhere on the field. Everyone needs to know where they are supposed to be and exactly what they are supposed to do. Real estate teams are the same. The real trick is getting the right people to play the right positions.

Teams are all about identity and brand. They hope to be easily recognized in their marketplace. It's not uncommon to see team photos in advertisements. A team takes pride in their ability to work as a unit. Teams want their individual identities to benefit the overall team identity.

If you are considering becoming part of an existing team, you will need to be able to show the team leader what position you are best able to play. If you are building a team, you will need to understand what cogs you will need to fill and be able to identify the best people to fill those spots. It isn't as easy as it appears.

Teams are also a great place for people who are not able to commit to Full-Service real estate sales because of other obligations. Rather than being fully responsible for every aspect of a real estate transaction, a team can offer specific roles. But this doesn't mean the team won't expect excellence in whatever they may do.

A team can benefit from Limited-Service agents who are able to provide on-demand administrative support, showing assistance or open house assistance. If the role and expectations are clearly defined, it could be a win-win for everyone involved. This is where a real estate coach can spot talent and abilities others might miss.

Real estate teams aren't the future – they are the present! There are some amazing success stories of real estate agents who have built incredible sales machines in this industry. The science of building these amazing sales collaboratives is growing. New methods for team efficiency are constantly being discovered.

If you are looking for something beyond solo sales, and something much more powerful than a real estate partnership, then consider a team. You can either build one or join one. No matter which path you take, you should spend some time talking with someone who can point you in the right direction. There are plenty of real estate teams looking for good people!

CHAPTER 9

Real Estate Groups

Real estate "teams" are today's hot sales trend. Real estate "groups" will be the next big thing on the horizon in this industry. A team and a group are not the same thing – not even close! Although both of these terms have been used interchangeably, they are two entirely different species of real estate sales collaboratives.

In the mid-1800s, the concept of the modern department store began to emerge in the United States. By the turn of the century, big-name department stores like Macy's started to change the way people shopped. The ability to shop for a wide range of products under a single roof was widely embraced by consumers. The same will happen in real estate!

The real estate industry will soon begin to move in a similar direction. Consumers will be attracted to real estate groups that offer a catalog of real estate services. The very best solo agents, partnerships and teams will be able to offer every imaginable service a real estate consumer might need. It sounds like a regular real estate office, but it isn't the same.

A real estate "group" will consist of sales professionals who choose to exist as a community of real estate service providers. Think of them as different departments in a department store. Each participant will offer a unique type and level of service. Real estate consumers will have a one-stop-shop opportunity with a "group".

There is one other major distinction between a team and a group. Every member of a *"team"* can only belong to one team. However, any member of one *"group"* can also be a part of another group. I know that sounds weird, but this underscores the distinct difference between these totally different real estate collaboratives.

A team offers "efficiency" of services. A group offers "diversity" of service. If a member offers a unique level of expertise or service, they could also be welcomed in many different groups and not offend any of the others in each group. Each group will welcome them because it adds to the depth and range of services they can all promote.

A team isn't likely to share talent in the same way because each member has a vital role as a cog in their sales machine. It would be like one baseball player being a member of multiple teams. It wouldn't make any sense. The chemistry of the team could also be compromised. If you are on a team, you should proudly wear the uniform and declare loyalty.

A group, on the other hand, consists of professionals who have carved out their own areas of expertise or service. They freely refer business within the group to other members who are better suited to serve a real estate consumer's need. Each member knows what they do well, and they gladly refer business to other members who can do it better than them.

Some areas of sales expertise could be new construction, land development, investments, flips, vacation homes, tax appeals, 1031 exchanges and so on. By having people in your group who specialize in these specific things, the depth of the group increases, and the consumers who need these services will be the beneficiaries.

A group instantly adds new tools to a member's real estate services toolbox. The more tools each member has, the more business they will get. A diverse group of quality agents and service providers could potentially have something to offer everyone. Participation in a diverse group of top producers offers a huge sales advantage.

This community of agents is like a company within a company. They all work under the same broker, but they maintain an internal sales comradery for the benefit of the group. The symbiotic energy of a group is important. Groups should be very selective about who can join their close-knit membership of industry professionals.

Steel sharpens steel, so it is important to work beside people who will also sharpen your sales performance. It is easy to become complacent when those around you have low expectations. A group maintains high standards and expects quality performance from everyone in the group. Don't join a group if you aren't serious about real estate.

A group also doesn't preclude newer agents from joining their ranks, but the expectations for them are also high. Highly motivated beginners bring a business-generating potential that allows these new recruits to strengthen the entire group and build business for everyone. Groups harness the energy of beginners, too!

So why doesn't a real estate group just become their own real estate company and cut out the broker? I know from first-hand experience that facilitating a group is nothing like managing your own real estate company. A good real estate office should help to build and develop groups. Running a company is much different than overseeing a collaborative!

It might seem logical to have everyone in the real estate company be required to be a part of one big group. That also won't work. Groups depend upon a balance of human chemistry. Just because a broker/owner wants to hire an agent, it doesn't mean that agent is the right fit for a group. Each group should have the final decision over its own membership.

A *"team"* is like a real estate sales tornado. A *"group"* is like a real estate services hurricane. There really is no comparison between these two sales collaboratives in terms of overall sales performance and expertise. A group is simply a force to be reckoned with in any marketplace.

Re/Max Achievers, Inc. has launched the very first real estate "group" in our area. I look forward to coaching this new group of real estate professionals. If you have exceptional real estate skills, experience or expertise, you should give us a call. If you are new to real estate, let us explain how a group could help you get started in sales.

CHAPTER 10

Commission Splits Changed Real Estate

Once upon a time, all real estate brokers split their commissions 50/50 with the agents. The broker provided the office, training, equipment and support staff to oversee the real estate deals, and the agents went out selling houses. It worked just fine for many decades; then everything changed!

In 1973 Dave Liniger, the man who founded Re/Max, broke the real estate commission paradigm when he started recruiting experienced, top performing real estate agents by giving them the entire commission pie. It worked, and it worked in a big way. Re/Max grew into one of the world's largest, international, mega-franchise.

Rather than splitting commissions between the broker and the agent, Re/Max began renting desk space and offering certain services to seasoned pros. They were already trained and experienced. These self-sufficient agents needed little support, other than professional office space and some administrative help.

Liniger changed the real estate business model in a drastic way. It was like a business philosophy meteor had struck our world and Dave's new model now threatened all the existing home sale dinosaurs. His model turned into an "adapt or die" reality for many of the old school real estate practitioners.

This new benchmark in the real estate commission timeline changed more than the share of money agents and brokers were putting into their pockets. It also changed what brokers were willing to invest into new agent development. Less commission income also meant less money for agent development and training.

The original Re/Max model wasn't designed for brand new real estate recruits to learn the business. Dave's model intentionally attracted seasoned, self-sufficient sales professionals. This model presumed the old school brokers who had always nurtured the next crop of agents would continue to do the same.

When the new recruits from training-minded agencies became top producing real estate professionals, they too packed up their bags and went to an office offering 100% commission splits. Who could blame them? It made perfect business sense for the agent, but literally no sense for the traditional, old-school training brokers.

Virtually all national franchise real estate companies followed with some version of the Re/Max 100% commission model. The independents soon did the same. They had no choice. It was the only way the other brokers could retain top producing agents. High commission split models eventually became the industry norm.

It's interesting how things eventually come full circle. Reduced agent training and development industry-wide is now becoming painfully obvious. Seasoned agents who are now retiring aren't being replaced by equally competent real estate recruits, because fewer offices are serving as true, new agent training centers.

In real estate, knowledge is power. The best real estate agents of the future will be the agents who have been trained and mentored by seasoned real estate brokers with a passion for agent development. I don't just mean sales. I also mean respectable business practices that build solid consumer and peer trust.

Re/Max is still perceived by some as a high-priced desk rental brokerage for experienced agents. Some believe it is not a comfortable place for new agents. Neither is true. Creative Re/Max commission split arrangements along with innovative training programs are emerging, serving as ideal incubators for newer agents.

The desk rental market also took a sharp turn when emerging technology enabled agents to work from home and much more efficiently from their smart phones. Today, fewer agents need the real estate office environment to run their business. Renting desk space to agents is quickly becoming a struggling business model.

The need for real estate education is increasing, and the need for desk space is decreasing. Another evolutionary shift appears to be on the real estate horizon! Those who are serious about becoming true real estate professionals must now shop for more than a 100% commission split and fancy office space.

Seasoned agents also need to relearn and rethink the way they do business. While they have been busy selling houses, the way real estate is transacted has changed drastically. The advent of collaborative sales models is expanding, and technology and social networks are changing the marketplace dynamics.

Teams and groups command their own commission split, negotiating power when they are affiliating with a broker. This is another reason more agents are migrating to these sales collaboratives. The power of sales volume can be beneficial to everyone who is part of high producing team or group.

Don't think the real estate offices of tomorrow will simply give away the ranch when it comes to real estate commissions. Do you remember what happened when Re/Max changed how the real estate pie was cut? Real estate brokers need to be compensated for quality agent training, problem-solving, collaborative engineering and more.

The real estate brokers of tomorrow will look much different than they do today. If you are a team or group that is looking to squeeze the life out of your real estate broker, you are missing the point. Commissions are only a part of the discussion and shouldn't be the bottom line. Focus on the value-added services and determine if the cost is truly fair.

Tomorrow's real estate broker needs to offer more than a desk, copier, fax machine and 100% commission splits. The new role of the broker serving as a trainer, mentor and career counselor is something to consider. You should be out selling homes while your real estate broker supports your role. If everyone does their part, the system works!

CHAPTER 11

Choosing Wide or Deep

The two "big dogs" when comparing national real estate franchises are Keller Williams and Re/Max. These massive real estate brokerage models are a perfect example of the real estate concept of being either wide or deep. Both mega-franchises will claim they are the biggest and best at what they do. Both are right!

Keller Williams has the greatest number of real estate licensees in the United States. They outnumber Re/Max licensees by a slim margin. If success were measured solely by the number of licenses on the wall of real estate offices, Keller Williams would be the winner. It's a notable accomplishment that earns them the distinction of being the "widest"!

Having the widest number of licensed real estate agents is the result of a brilliant multi-level commission model. Real estate agents within Keller Williams franchises can earn additional income by recruiting more agents into the KW organization. Recruiting new agents earns existing agents a piece of every commission dollar generated by the new folks they recruit.

I love innovators! Gary Keller and Joe Williams launched their real estate model nearly a decade after Dave Liniger, the founding father of Re/Max. Over the past 35 years, this KW duo has made their mark as one of the big dogs in the real estate marketplace. They are undoubtedly the biggest and the best at what they set out to do, but so is Re/Max!

If you recall what I said about the birth of the Re/Max franchise in Chapter 10, remember that Dave Liniger recruited the very best top-producing real estate agents through his 100% commission model. It worked like a charm, and the results of his efforts are evident through different statistics, which makes Re/Max the "deepest" of these giants.

Although KW agents are more plentiful than Re/Max agents, they lack the tenured depth of their Re/Max counterparts. The KW multi-level commission program understandably attracts newer agents. Conversely, the Re/Max franchises continues to attract a more seasoned real estate sales force that tend to dominate a marketplace.

The statistical proof of the professional depth found at Re/Max versus KW is seen through the average income and transaction stats on an individual agent basis. An average Re/Max agent earns far more income than a KW agent. Although KW is winning the licensee race, they are still lagging behind in the average income per agent race.

All of this statistical bantering about the two big dogs isn't the point of this chapter! The question of width or depth is relevant in whatever real estate office you may choose. Not every Re/Max or KW franchise has the same depth when analyzed at the office level. The management and chemistry of the sales associates in each office determines their true depth.

I want you to think of the concept of wide and deep as it relates to a river. A "wide" river is often a shallow river. In the best of times, these rivers are just deep enough to comfortably accommodate passage. However, when a drought occurs, the widest rivers are also prone to becoming even more shallow. They can dry up very quickly.

A "deep" river is usually narrower than the wide rivers. Their depth isn't as obvious and impressive from the surface, but it also isn't as susceptible to drought. A deep river can withstand the dry season. In the best of times this may not seem like a big deal, but it is really quite important. Real estate markets, just like rivers, can be vulnerable during droughts.

When you are considering which real estate office will be the best place for you, there are many options – not just Re/Max and Keller Williams. When you are looking at other offices, you need to be able to recognize the difference between wide and deep. If you plan to be in real estate for the long haul, knowing the difference could be a matter of survival.

A wide real estate brokerage is a place where a wide number of minimally experienced agents all compete for the same customers. Business is spread thin! If you are in an office where all the agents are grappling for the same single-family residential customers, you will wish you were in deeper waters when times get tough – and it will happen!

A deep real estate brokerage has seasoned real estate professionals with a wide range of real estate expertise. This is a place where knowledge, skills and tools are practiced and developed continually. Learning is as important to the seasoned agents as it is to the newer agents. A perfect example is Donna Russell's insatiable appetite to keep learning after 25 years!

This broad spectrum of expertise attracts more clients to these types of brokerages. In Chapter 9 I wrote about real estate "groups". The core philosophy behind a group is the collective depth of knowledge and expertise of the participants. A group is designed to be deeper than it is wide. It isn't about the number of participants, it's about their depth!

New agents are sometimes intimidated by the deep waters of a real estate office filled with seasoned agents. That's stinking thinking – it's a misconception. Every new agent should jump at the chance to work shoulder to shoulder with seasoned sales pros. You will compete with them in the marketplace whether you are in the same office, or not!

As I moved from one office to another in my own career path, width and depth were key factors in my office considerations. When you are interviewing with a real estate office, ask the manager or recruiter to tell you about the depth of their office. If you take the time to meet with me, I'll show you what this conversation should look like.

CHAPTER 12

Part-Time and Limited-Service Agents

It isn't easy to get started as a full-time real estate professional, especially if you are the main bread winner in your household. Making a living solely on commissions requires a major leap of faith, some money in the bank and the backing of a real estate broker who can help you achieve your goals.

Even with these things in place, you could still find yourself crossing the financial desert for a time. Some agents can go as many as 3 – 4 months before they see their first real estate commission check. Even then, the cash flow may not be consistent for several more months.

The solution for many real estate sales hopefuls is to work another full-time job while they start to grow their real estate prospect database. That's what I did. It took me one full year to gain the financial momentum to leave my regular day job in 1989 and subsequently start my new real estate career. I'm not sorry I took this career path.

I made my career jump thirty years ago when practicing real estate was much less complicated than it is today. Brokers in those days offered more services because we split our commissions 50/50. Today's 100% commission splits and per-transaction fee arrangements make part-time real estate career start-ups more difficult. It's harder than ever to get started in real estate!

What determines if a real estate agent is either "full-time" or "part-time"? It's much easier to classify them as "full-service" or "limited-service" agents. There is a big difference. It doesn't matter how much time they are willing to invest in our profession. What matters most is the quality of service and support they can offer!

Problem arises when part-time agents claim they are full-service agents but they are inexperienced and unavailable – especially if they are solo agents! This is a big problem for real estate consumers, as well as their full-service real estate peers who must try to compensate for the inefficiency and incompetency on the other side of a real estate deal.

Agents who claim to be full-service agents because they don't work another full-time job may not truly be full-service agents. Their personal commitments or other interests can interfere with their ability to offer full-service customer care, as well. It's about the level of service, not the time invested, that is the defining characteristic that matters most.

If you cannot readily be available to consumers and fellow agents, that doesn't mean there is no place for you in real estate sales. You still have a few other options to consider instead of giving up your dream to sell real estate. You could be the missing part in a real estate collaborative, as I have described, or even a great real estate technician or assistant.

Another possibility is becoming a "limited-service agent". This means the real estate services you will personally offer to consumers is "limited" to a few specific tasks requiring a real estate license. You won't do it all. Although you are legally licensed to perform certain sales duties, you willingly agree to refrain from performing certain tasks.

A limited-service agent can host open houses, serve as a showing host and actively prospect for business and develop leads. They cannot prepare contracts, present contracts, give property valuations and many other duties for consumers, which require proficiency through repetition. They can be paid hourly or by referral fees for their efforts.

Those who start their careers as limited-service agents feel a sense of relief because they are not expected to perform complicated sales duties. Limited-service agents are also in a great position to learn from the full-service agents and be mentored. They can develop the confidence to eventually make the big step to a full-service career in real estate.

Limited-service agents fill a big void for the full-service agents who need additional help to show homes and host open houses from time to time. This gives full-service agents some licensed assistance and also gives the limited-service agent some real-life experience in working with real clients. It's good for everyone involved.

These working arrangements can also lead to partnerships or invitations to join real estate sales teams. It gets your foot in the door. It gives you a chance to get to know the different real estate professionals in your office. You will be able to tell if you have the right chemistry for different collaborative sales relationships.

Part time agents who pretend to be full-service real estate professionals give the real estate industry a bad name. In my opinion, it is a terrible business practice to represent yourself as something you are not. Sadly, some consumers don't realize this important service distinction until they are under contract for services with a solo, part-time agent!

There is a legitimate way to be a part-time contributor in a profession that requires full-service attention. Your real estate broker or manager should help you understand this process. Limited-service agency is an option that wasn't available or feasible when I started in real estate. Times have changed!

CHAPTER 13

The Missing Parts

It doesn't take new real estate agents very long to realize what they don't know. Real estate is a complex business. It's hard to look and feel confident when you are just starting your sales career. Most real estate consumers can quickly sense if an agent is in over their head when confronted with a complex question.

Don't give up hope! Just because you can't do it all or know it all, this doesn't mean that you can't do anything. Some people excel in certain areas of real estate, but they never reach their full sales potential because of the few skills they are unable to master. You could be the missing part a real estate collaborative desperately needs!

Real estate career consultants keep an open eye for missing parts to strengthen their firm's collaboratives. When interviewing with a real estate company, ask about the collaborative opportunities in their office. Whether you are brand new to this business or looking for a fresh start, this is an important question to ask!

Some real estate brokers leave the collaborative-building duties entirely to the partnerships, teams and groups. Why? It's because they are all independent contractors and they probably get a very favorable commission split. But times are changing, and today's brokers are increasingly a part of helping to engineer these new-age sales entities.

If you have floundered in real estate sales for years, collaboratives could be an option for you to consider! You could be the essential ingredient some real estate partnership, team or group needs in their recipe for success. I have seen many quality people leave this industry simply because no one helped them find a comfortable place to fit.

The real estate industry has more roles to fill than ever before. Whether you are filling an unlicensed role or you are licensed to sell, the right spot for you could be out there. But the real estate collaboratives need to know about your unique skills and background. If you can't sell yourself, then you need to find someone who can promote you!

Successful real estate collaboratives sell houses; they don't actively scout for talent. If a partnership, team or group gets a taste for what you have to offer, you could have a chance at becoming an essential cog in their sales machine or services department store. If you have a strong professional background, you will attract the attention of a group.

Your gifts, talents and passions have value. A place to fit can provide you with more income, as well as improved personal self-esteem. A real estate career counselor will help you assess your personal strengths and weaknesses. Please take the time to talk with someone who may be able to see things in you that you simply can't see in yourself.

The entire real estate industry loses when a good match is lost. The real estate partnerships, teams and groups will never know the individual they desperately need has just sent their license back to Harrisburg into a sea of inactive licenses. We all need quality parts!

Whether you are just starting or are ready to quit, please think about what I am saying in this chapter. Take the time to speak with a real estate career counselor. Talk to someone who is trained to assess your strengths and talents. The perfect place for you may not be available immediately. You will need to be patient and wait for that big opportunity.

If you are a team or a group looking for people to add to your real estate sales collaborative, you should also think about these words. Do you have a real estate parts matchmaker? You should be out there selling homes and leave the talent recruiting to your broker or the career counselor in the office. Who is filling this essential role where you currently work?

CHAPTER 14

Who Needs A License Anyway?

Not every task in real estate sales requires a real estate license. For those considering a career in this industry, think about starting as a real estate technician or administrative assistant, rather than a licensed sales professional. You can get a paycheck, learn the real estate business and eventually work on obtaining a license.

Salespeople only get paid if the buyer buys or the seller sells. They are willing to gamble their time and energy on real estate consumers with the hope they will be paid at settlement. If and when the deal gets to the settlement table, salespeople are paid handsomely. Some folks don't like taking this risk.

In contrast, real estate technicians and administrative assistants perform tasks for licensed real estate professionals that do not fall under the duties that can only be performed by a licensee. Real estate techs and assistants are paid for the work they perform, either by the hour or by a set fee for specific tasks. It's sure money.

There is a distinct difference between a technician and an assistant. A technician is typically an independent contractor and an assistant is usually an employee. One is a 1099 wage earner, and the other is usually a W-2 employee. Choosing the right role depends on many different factors for both parties.

Having someone work on an as-needed basis bodes well for some real estate professionals. The ebb and flow of sales income affects our need for regular hourly assistance. The downside of an on-demand contractor is the possibility that our favorite technician may not be available during the times when we need them the most.

Being a technician has several benefits. It's a great way to see if they like working with an individual agent or team before committing to a position as an employee. It's also a great way to learn the real estate business and get paid at the same time. Great technicians have the potential to become great salespeople one day.

An assistant is often a trusted employee with stable work hours and consistency in the type of work that is done on a daily basis. It's a regular day job. These folks like the predictability of this type of working arrangement. But when sales are slow, the need is low, and job security can become a risk factor for assistants.

Administrative assistants are usually great paperwork people. They are detail-oriented and provide the organizational skills that many top producing real estate agents often lack. They can bring valuable legal, marketing, advertising or social media expertise to help agents who lack these special skills.

Real estate technicians usually offer a broader range of services. It could be photography, graphic design, writing, social media, marketing research, administrative skills, technology or any other tasks that could benefit a salesforce. They are much more likely to work night and weekend hours for an extra fee.

Technicians who lack the technical skills I just mentioned may have time and energy as their biggest asset. Salespeople also need help putting up signs and taking them down, restocking highlight sheets, delivering paperwork, handyman help and other behind the scenes duties that can consume an agent's schedule.

Technicians are encouraged to learn industry-specific skills like real estate document preparation, paperwork review, transaction tracking, data research and more. These services are performed directly for the agent. Direct communications with real estate consumers is not permitted unless you are licensed.

Real estate technicians and administrative assistants should both take real estate classes to learn industry-specific duties to make them more marketable to salespeople. After a basic class, they need to keep learning additional skills that will add to their unlicensed real estate services toolbox and broaden their own marketability.

If techs are good at what they do, they will be solicited by top producing agents, teams or groups. That's great! Their hard work should pay off and they will be compensated nicely when their skills are developed. They also have the option to remain independent and simply increase their fees as demand for them increases.

Another great aspect of being a real estate technician or administrative assistant is the ability to work remotely from a home office. Depending upon their current life circumstances, this career choice is an ideal home business opportunity that enables them to work at home and tend to other family obligations.

You may be determined to remain a solo, independent agent throughout your real estate career. Solo agents who want to remain independent, without paying an assistant, should consider hiring a real estate technician. This added resource allows you to focus on business-generating activity and delegate other tasks.

Those of you who have a team or group should also keep this on-demand resource on your radar screen. Real estate technicians can be the additional moving parts that accomplish much-needed tasks without committing to a full-time employee. It's also a great way to test some new talent for your collaborative.

If your real estate career has gone nowhere, this may be a viable alternative. Just because your sales career didn't get off the ground, it doesn't mean there isn't a place for you in real estate. I spoke about missing parts in Chapter 13. Real estate technicians and assistants are often an essential missing part!

If you have an inactive real estate license, you may want to check to see if you can still revive it within the five-year reactivation window. Rather than allowing your license to expire, you can have the best of both worlds by serving as a real estate technician or assistant, as well as earning referral commissions. Your options are limitless!

CHAPTER 15

The Problem-Solving Business

Real estate is a problem-solving business!

Few of us think about the real 911 dispatchers, waiting there day and night, ready to send help in a true emergency. Likewise, many real estate agents and collaboratives don't consider who will be there, ready to respond, when they have a real estate transaction 911 situation. This is an important factor to consider when you are broker shopping!

When my daughter decided to follow my footsteps into real estate sales, "problem-solving business" were the first words she heard from my mouth. I wasn't trying to discourage her from selling homes, as I had also done for decades. I was preparing her for the crisis management nature of this business. Problems are plentiful in real estate.

Buying a home is the biggest financial decision most people will make in their lifetime. For many, it's a 30-year obligation. Quality agents truly care about their clients. When a real estate deal is going bad, thousands of dollars are on the line for the client. It can become emotional and nerve wracking. That's when you need qualified and accessible help!

Real estate problems come in all shapes and sizes, and they can occur even if you have done everything properly. Most problems are resolved when calm minds prevail. Unfortunately, some real estate issues can turn into real nightmares. Your clients will feel much better knowing you have a reliable transaction crisis back-up plan.

When you are shopping for a real estate brokerage, crisis management should be high on your list. Your broker and manager will be your lifeline when a real estate calamity unfolds. If I were personally looking for a new company affiliation, crisis management assistance would be a top priority.

I counsel agents who are considering a new broker affiliation. Rarely do these prospects inquire about the critical response support they will receive. Only experienced agents who have previously been swept away in a legal liability riptide will want to know more about this valuable support.

Likewise, real estate recruiters who are trying to lure agents to join their company rarely boast about their crisis management. The other shiny bells and whistles tend to draw an agent's attention away from this essential resource. You should poll some of the current agents in each company you interview on this topic!

The legal insight from my past brokers or managers were valuable to me when I occasionally found myself, or my clients, stuck in transactional quicksand. Another great resource in times of trouble are the experienced professional around you. This is another power benefit of a real estate group that naturally attracts experienced agents.

Proper training, quality contract reviews and good documentation are the best way to limit legal liability. But no matter what you do, sometimes you can get into a legal jam. When this happens, you will be sounding a transactional 911 alarm. If you have carefully screened the critical response team in the office where you work, you'll be OK!

Real estate agents aren't just paid to guide people through houses. We are also there to guide our clients through a maze of potential problems and legal pitfalls. We are compensated well for what we do, and what we are paid to do is to prevent and solve problems for our customers and clients to the best of our ability.

CHAPTER 16

Curiosity for Sale

Where do most real estate leads originate? They originate in the minds of consumers who are curious about their housing options. Curiosity is the catalyst that sets most real estate transactions into motion. Today these curious minds are unwittingly identified on-line and then sold to waiting real estate agents. Consumers are captured and sold as leads.

Real estate agents have been buying and selling real estate referral leads for decades. It's a good source of potential business for full-service agents. Rather than spending their own time and money in search of people who are interested in buying, selling or renting real estate, top agents purchase real estate prospect information.

Most agents will gladly pay anywhere from 25% to 33% of their commission for a lead that is converted into a closed deal. In the early days of real estate, brokers made a good living selling out-of-town leads. With the advent of the internet, the real estate franchises that once specialized in these types of referrals slowly disappeared.

Then in 2006 two Microsoft executives founded a company you may know. It's called Zillow. These two guys thought they could mine real estate leads on-line and subsequently sell them to real estate agents. They were right! They built a lead machine unlike any had ever done before, and their lead stream became a raging river. They learned to sell curiosity!

I have argued for years that someone who focused solely on lead generating could make a great living doing just that – no listing, no selling, no showings, no settlements… just mining leads and selling them to other agents. Zillow proved my theory to be correct. And you don't need a license to do market research!

The Zillow start-up venture quickly turned the age-old practice of selling real estate referral leads into what is today - a $2.5 billion-dollar business model. They figured out how to do it right. Newer real estate agents didn't need to learn the art of turning prospects into contacts and contacts into leads. They just bought them.

The fact that Zillow struck real estate referral gold merely proves the real estate lead business is both worthwhile and lucrative. Zillow isn't keeping others from doing the same! In fact, some of the best real estate days are ahead for the agents and teams who learn the timeless art of mining for their own real estate consumer leads.

It is not uncommon for real estate brokerages to have their own real estate referral networks. Some of them are nothing more than a real estate license graveyard where agents who couldn't figure out how to make money eventually hang their license. In Chapter 18 we will take a look at The Spectrum Networks and offer a different perspective.

The Spectrum Networks provide real estate agents who no longer want to pay real estate association dues or MLS fees with a great alternative. This company is uniquely different from its referral counterparts because agents from any real estate firm can build their referral network there. There is no monthly or yearly fee to hang a license!

The real purpose of a referral company is to create a lead stream for full-service agents. Many of these referral endeavors are not properly funded, managed or promoted. Some produce a few meager leads per year, which barely justifies their existence. If you are in this type of hopeless referral arrangement - get out now!

Whether you are a new agent or seasoned agent aspiring to reach a higher sales plateau, you need to master the science of building good lead streams. Consider building your own referral network that you can personally manage and keep, even if you move from broker to broker, as many agents do.

If you are reaching the point in your career when you feel it is time to hang up your license entirely, think again! Referrals are a great way to continue to earn some serious income by leveraging your own personal and professional spheres. But there is a real science to keeping long-time business spheres alive.

Innovative real estate sales collaboratives should also consider the value of employing a lead stream specialist as a part of their home sales machines.

When you add up the costs you are paying for these on-line prospects, you might find a better value and higher quality lead by paying someone to do it better for you.

Zillow burst onto the real estate scene a little more than a decade ago. Their influence has continued to grow and with good reason. The art and science of lead generating is not taught in the few offices that still provide quality real estate sales training. Our industry is now completely addicted to the third-party lead prospectors.

The crazy part is that nothing has changed! It has been said that curiosity killed the cat – but curiosity is what made Zillow fat! The leads we are buying from them are nothing more than curious consumers who are surfing the internet when they begin to feel the urge to find a new home. It's the same thing we have all done with Open Houses for many decades!

I have heard old school real estate brokers describe Zillow and the other national lead specialists as poachers or as an invasive species that is ruining our industry. Not true! These innovative business entrepreneurs have recognized our decreasing skill and the increased laziness among real estate professionals. Good for them!

Can ordinary real estate sales people really compete with these real estate lead mining giants? Absolutely! In fact, we have a distinct advantage over them. However, our advantage will only be realized when agents, old and new, return to school to learn more about the art and science of prospecting for leads.

Brokers need to teach the lead stream sciences and provide modern referral platforms like The Spectrum Networks where agents can launch their own referral networks. Your real estate career can reach new productivity levels, or you may find your own niche role in the real estate marketplace if you learn to mine and sell your leads to waiting agents.

CHAPTER 17

Do You Use An S-GPS?

One of the major steps along your real estate career pathway is called a "performance plateau" mentioned in Chapter 4. This occurs when your sales volume reaches a glass ceiling that you cannot seem to break. This performance barrier seems impenetrable. This is where a real estate S-GPS can come to the rescue!

A "Global Positioning System" tells us where we are located and how to get where we want to go. In real estate, the term S-GPS stands for "Sales Generating Point System" and it can basically do the same thing for your real estate sales performance as the GPS in your car.

I was lost and frustrated when I started on my own sales career path. Back then, the GPS systems hadn't been invented, either for cars or for real estate agents. So, I built my own real estate S-GPS for my financial sanity. It was a trial and error development process, but I eventually achieved the results I was seeking.

In the years to follow, my real estate S-GPS became a trusted guide to help me understand my sales volume and understand how to get where I wanted to go. I can't imagine selling real estate without it. When my daughter started selling real estate, my real estate S-GPS model was a part of her real estate sales orientation.

Over the past three decades, I have made a few modifications to my system as new technologies and social media evolved. For the most part the core operating principles are fundamentally unchanged since the late 1980s. These foundational concepts are timeless and still relevant in real estate today.

My real estate S-GPS also became the standard I used when managing real estate salespeople, and it was the teaching model for all the agents I trained. It was the only way I could accurately assess how they were progressing along their real estate career path and what needed to be done to reach their next performance plateau.

Some of the agents I trained balked at my system. They liked doing their own thing and did not like being told how to sell. I never forced anyone to use my real estate S-GPS because it doesn't work if you don't fully embrace the concept. But I also couldn't offer them much help or assurance if they chose to freelance.

I'm a numbers person. I love analytics. When I created my real estate S-GPS I fully believed sales productivity was the result of quantifiable actions. I was right. Certain things we do will result in greater sales volumes. If we control these measurable actions, we will see measurable results. It's a simple concept.

Real estate agents who are trapped in a sales performance plateau want to see measurable change in their sales volume. It can be done! By simply changing what you are doing, you can change what you are making. But changing what we are doing also means changing certain habits and behaviors we tightly embrace.

Years after I developed my own real estate S-GPS, Weight Watchers developed a point system for weight loss. They embraced the concept of creating measurable change through a point-based rewarded system for certain behaviors and foods consumed. Point systems are a universally accepted approach in many disciplines.

I created my point system to control my own sales productivity. I was a solo agent back then. As the new age of collaborative home sales dawned, I had the opportunity to modify my point system to be used by real estate sales teams. It worked as effectively with multiple people as it did with the lone sales practitioners.

Every analytics enthusiast believes their formulas and metrics are the best; I'm no exception. What I developed worked well for me, and it worked for the real estate agents I trained and the teams I coached. The only exception, when my system didn't produce results, was when agents didn't follow the program precisely.

If you have some degree of natural sales ability, you will reach your own natural sales performance plateau. You may wonder how some of these top producing real estate superstars produce at incredible sales performance levels.

They all have one thing in common - they all follow their own system and they stick to it.

The secret sauce behind every successful point system is not simply changing your behavior but also adopting a new mindset. Your mindset is the foundation beneath your behaviors. It isn't just about what you do but also about why you do it. Performance plateaus cannot be overcome by merely hoping for change.

My point system also wasn't money-based. Sure, I needed to make money, but I had an even greater passion. I was driven to be able to spend time at my place on the lake with my wife and kids. When I reached my designated point total for the week, the family and I were cleared to head to the Poconos without any guilt.

I knew how many points I needed to earn per week to financially support my family. My wife also knew my point goals. She was my cheerleader throughout the week as I generated my points, because she also wanted to spend the weekend at the lake as much as I did. My points ultimately earned me the family time I treasured.

The point system I have created for real estate certainly isn't the only sales performance system in this industry. It worked for me, and maybe it could work for you. If you are currently camped out in a sales performance plateau and you want to pull up stakes and move to the next level, find a system that works for you!

CHAPTER 18

The Spectrum Networks

To appreciate the failure rate in real estate sales, simply talk to the folks at the Pennsylvania Department of State. At any given time, more than 100,000 real estate licenses are in the 5-year expiration pile. The hard work these folks invested to obtain their license is about to be lost.

If you are one of those people who has a real estate license that was sent back to Harrisburg, I encourage you to read this chapter carefully. If you are a full-service licensee, you should ear-mark this chapter. The next time you are looking for more business, you should re-read this chapter.

The real estate inactive licensee recycle bin is a gold mine of potential leads! Calculate the success rate of the prospects you are purchasing from the on-line lead hucksters. You won't be impressed! You should consider the most highly successful lead stream of all – personal referrals.

A personal referral comes with something you can't buy from the on-line curiosity traplines – credibility. A lead that originates from someone the consumer knows and trusts is a great lead, not merely a prospect who may or may not be looking for real estate services. A personal referral also comes with a personal endorsement.

Those who tried and failed at real estate sales may not be able to master the real estate task juggling act, but they do have the one thing that matters most in real estate: they have a sphere of influence! They are associated with people with whom they have favor, influence, recognition, satisfaction and trust. They can put you FIRST in line!

One of the emotional gut-punches you could face when you are newly licensed is when friends and family choose to use another real estate agent over you. It happens to all of us and for a good reason. The people in your sphere of influence recognize you are brand new and realize you literally know nothing about real estate. Why shouldn't they go elsewhere?

Although the folks in your sphere of influence may not trust your real estate sales expertise, they would surely like to get a break on the cost of their real estate services. Full-service licensees will gladly pay anywhere from 25% - 33% for a ready, willing and able real estate consumer.

If a referral agent has a friend who is about to purchase a $300,000 home, the buyer agent could potentially receive a $9,000 commission on the buyer's side. If they pay a 25% commission the referral company will receive $2,250. The total due to the referral agent after company fees will be approximately $1,687.

The referral agent can receive a check for the entire $1,687, or they can credit part of their commission back to the buyer at settlement, just like a traditional real estate agent could. Their friend could get $1,000 toward their closing costs at settlement and the referral agent could make $687. It's a win-win for everyone involved.

If a referral agent isn't interested in helping a friend, and they really don't need the money themselves, there is another good option. Non-profit agencies across the country are strapped for cash. How many times do churches, school associations, Relay for Life and other charities get a single donation as high as $1,687?

If you are a full-service or referral agent who belongs to one of these non-profits – listen up! Real estate referral monies that are donated directly to an approved charity at the time of settlement could make a big difference for unfortunate people or charitable groups that desperately need the funds.

You have this book because I mentioned I would like to sit down and speak with you sometime. This may be a talking point that has caught your attention. I will share the story of a family who shared a big check with Children's Hospital of Philadelphia through this very program. You could do the same for other organizations!

The full-service agent in my earlier example made $6,750 on a real estate transaction they would have otherwise never had in their sales pipeline. It doesn't take long for these types of leads to add up into big numbers. Full-service agents can benefit from a great lead stream.

I previously mentioned The Spectrum Networks. This is a real estate referral company that allows agents from any company to build their real estate referral network. Spectrum doesn't charge a monthly or yearly fee for someone to hang their license on the wall. People with inactive real estate licenses don't need to pay any fees.

Referral agents do need to take real estate continuing education bi-annually. The Spectrum Networks also has another great feature: if the referral agent has provided at least one successful real estate referral within the 2-year continuing education timeframe, the CE classes needed for their renewal are also FREE!

An inactive licensee must also invest the time and money to reactivate their license. Full-service licensees can use this as an investment opportunity. Helping to get someone back into the business as a referral agent by sharing these costs can pay big dividends through the lead stream prospects that are unleashed.

The Spectrum Networks is also run like an off-shore referral option. I don't literally mean out of the country, but I do mean out of the reach of a traditional broker's office. It is not uncommon for full-service licensees to make a few moves in their career. When these moves occur, the agent's referral network is often left behind at their prior broker's office.

I was personally involved with the creation of The Spectrum Networks. This company was designed just as I have described because the real estate referral business has never really received the recognition it deserves as a rich source of real estate business. Instead, we continue allow the good people at Zillow to sell us low quality prospects.

As we near the end of this book, I hope you are beginning to see things that you never considered before. This is the reason I have taken the time to write this book. There is a whole world of possibilities that you may have never realized in the past. If you have reached this point in the book, you must surely have a few new insights.

CHAPTER 19

Where Do We Go from Here?

I started this book with this sentiment, and I will share it again. If you are happy where you are, you would be crazy to consider making a move! Plenty of agents are satisfied with their income, management, training and the chemistry of people in their company. If you are content – please, stay where you are!

This book is shared with people I hope to meet and eventually talk with some day. That's you! Whether you would be a good fit for Re/Max Achievers or we are the type of company you have been seeking remains to be seen. But you do have something I truly want – your perspective!

I have covered a wide variety of topics in this short book. As you can tell, I have my own thoughts and opinions on these matters. You have listened to what I have to say by reading my book. I would now like to hear your thoughts. I value your perspective. I want to know how you see it, whether you agree with me or not.

These books are often shared with agents who have worked on transactions with some of the real estate professionals at Re/Max Achievers. Our agents tell us about the cooperating agents who stand above the rest in terms of professional expertise, customer service and overall communications skills. Maybe that's you!

If you have never worked with someone in the Re/Max Achievers office, you may present yourself in the marketplace with a level of professionalism that has caught our eye. You may stand above the rest. It isn't hard to spot those who have worked diligently to build their identity or brand in our marketplace.

Some of you are real estate sales hopefuls or totally new agents. You are unproven in this profession. You offer a fresh perspective that has not been influenced by this industry. We want to hear how you see this business through a fresh set of eyes. Your insight is also valuable to me and my industry research.

Finally, there are you folks who have run the good race. You have reached the end of your real estate career. For one reason or another, it is time to call it quits. Tell me how you plan to do it! Retirement is one of the greatest mysteries of the real estate profession. I am still looking for the perfect solution, but I do have some good options.

This is certainly not the last book I plan to write about the real estate profession. For one reason or another, I believe you may have the perspective, insight or wisdom I might want to include in my future writing. That's why we need to talk. I want to pick your brain for my future writing endeavors.

Building teams and groups are my passion. Finding the right pieces that fit together and work like a finely tuned machine is the second most rewarding thing I do, aside from my teaching. When a team or group comes alive and functions like they sometimes have the potential to do, it is a proud moment for me. We should talk.

I could have written many more chapters in this book. I never intended for this to be a book in the first place. I have narrowed down the subject matter, so it would give us a baseline for future conversations. I hope this book and these topics have evoked some thoughts that we can discuss sometime.

You have given me a little more than an hour of your time to read this material. I am sincerely grateful. Even if we never meet or talk, I hope you have found something in these pages that is helpful to you and your real estate career. Maybe my thoughts will inspire you to write a book of your own.

On behalf of me, John Ohler, Nicole Roman and everyone at Re/Max Achievers, we wish you the very best at whatever point you find yourself on your real estate career path. Thanks again for taking your valuable time to read our book.

We truly hope to hear from you!

Randal S. Doaty
(610) 858-3524 – mobile phone or text
rdoaty@doaty.com – direct e-mail